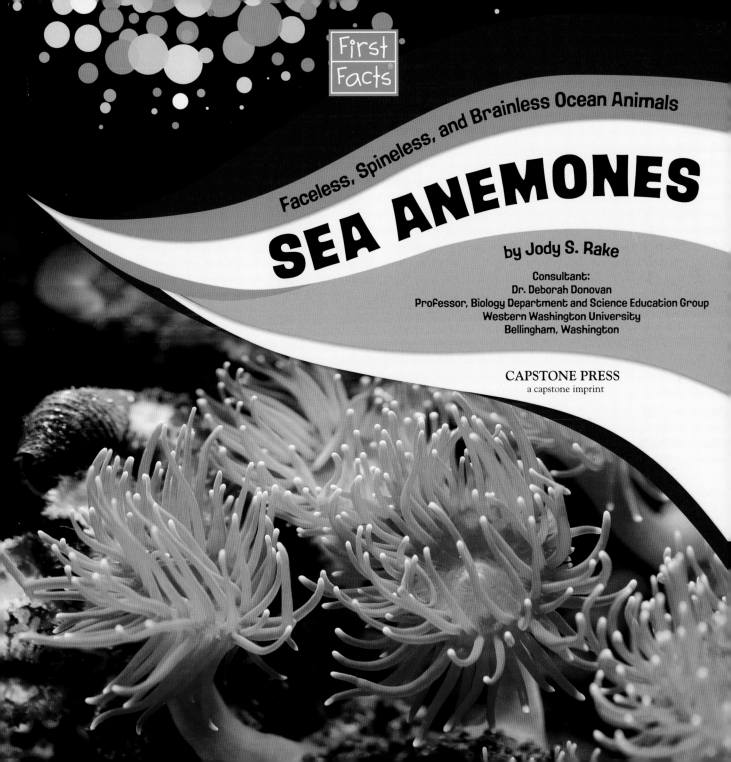

First Facts®

Faceless, Spineless, and Brainless Ocean Animals

# SEA ANEMONES

by Jody S. Rake

Consultant:
Dr. Deborah Donovan
Professor, Biology Department and Science Education Group
Western Washington University
Bellingham, Washington

CAPSTONE PRESS
a capstone imprint

First Facts are published by Capstone Press,
1710 Roe Crest Drive, North Mankato, Minnesota 56003
www.mycapstone.com

**Library of Congress Cataloging-in-Publication Data**
Names: Rake, Jody Sullivan, author.
Title: Sea anemones / by Jody S. Rake.
Description: North Mankato, Minnesota : Capstone Press, [2017] | Series: First facts. Brainless,
    spineless, and faceless ocean animals | Audience: Ages 7-9._ | Audience: K to grade 3._ |
    Includes bibliographical references and index. | Description based on print version record
     and CIP data provided by publisher; resource not viewed.
Identifiers: LCCN 2016001226 (print) | LCCN 2015051438 (ebook) | ISBN 9781515721475
    (eBook PDF) | ISBN 9781515721390 (hardcover) | ISBN 9781515721437 (pbk.)
Subjects: LCSH: Sea anemones—Juvenile literature. | Marine animals—Juvenile literature.
Classification: LCC QL377.C7 (print) | LCC QL377.C7 S87 2017 (ebook) | DDC 593.6—dc23
LC record available at http://lccn.loc.gov/2016001226

**Editorial Credits**
Abby Colich, editor; Bobbie Nuytten, designer; Kelly Garvin, media researcher; Steve Walker,
production specialist

**Photo Credits**
Newscom: Educational Images Ltd/Custom Medical Stock Photo "CMSP Biology", 11, Image
Quest 3-D/NHPA/Photoshot, 19; Shutterstock: Andrey Armyagov, 17, Jung Hsuan, 20,
Konstantin Novikov, 13, NatureDiver, 9, 21, Offscreen, cover, 1, rosesmith, 6, shaferaphoto, 15,
Stas Moroz, 7, tgunal, 5

Artistic Elements:
Shutterstock: Artishok, Vikasuh

Printed and bound in China

PO007692RRDF16

# Table of Contents

# Life without Bones

Did you know that there are animals without backbones? Animals with no backbone, or spine, are **invertebrates**. Sea anemones are invertebrates. They have no face or brain either. Other body parts help them move and find food.

invertebrate—an animal without a backbone

# A Sea of Anemones

There are more than 1,000 **species** of sea anemones. They live in every ocean of the world. Some live near **coral reefs**. They prefer the warm, shallow water found there. Others live in colder, deeper water.

Sea anemones can be many sizes. The smallest ones are less than 0.5 inch (1.3 centimeters) wide. Large ones can grow up to 6 feet (1.8 meters) wide. Most are about the size of a teacup.

**Fact!** The sea anemone is named after the anemone flower.

**species**—a group of creatures that are capable of reproducing with one another

**coral reef**—a part of the seafloor made up of the hardened bodies of corals; corals are small, colorful sea creatures

# Pretty as a Flower

Most sea anemones look like flowers. Colorful **tentacles** surround this animal's mouth. The tentacles often look like flower petals. Others look like fingers or spaghetti. Some even look like fur.

Under the tentacles is a tube-shaped body, or column. At the bottom of the body is the pedal disc. The pedal disc lets the anemone move or stay in place.

**tentacle**—a long, armlike body part of some animals

**algae**—small plantlike organisms without roots or stems that grow in water or on damp surfaces

## Colors in the Sea

Sea anemones come in every color. Most are the same color as their parents. They also get colors in other ways. Anemones that eat shrimp look red. Some anemones have **algae** growing in their tentacles. The algae make them look green or brown.

# Bring on the Sting

They may look pretty, but a sea anemone's tentacles are dangerous. Some animals come by and think the tentacles are food. Then zap! The tentacles sting the **prey**. The prey can no longer move. Then the tentacles move the prey into the anemone's mouth.

Most sea anemones eat other invertebrates. They may munch on crabs or shrimp. Small anemones gulp tiny **plankton**. Large anemones eat fish.

## Stingers, Darts, and Other Parts

A sea anemone's stinger is tiny. Its sting comes from a special cell in the tentacle. Each cell holds a sharp dart. The dart carries **venom**. When prey touches the stinger, the dart fires. It shoots venom into the prey.

**prey**—an animal hunted by another animal for food
**plankton**—tiny organisms that drift in the sea
**venom**—a poison an animal makes to kill its prey

11

# Sticking Around

The anemone's pedal disc works like a suction cup. The disc helps the animal stay put. When it needs to move, the anemone uses the disc to slowly creep along. Some anemones completely let go of a surface and roll away. Others even flip over and "walk" on their tentacles!

**Fact!** Sea anemones are closely related to jellyfish. Some species look like an upside-down jellyfish.

pedal disc

# The Nerve Net

Sea anemones don't have brains. Instead they have a system of **nerves**. Nerves surround the body like a net. They let the animal move its tentacles or attach to rocks. They also help the anemone find food and eat.

**Fact!** Sea anemones are not currently **endangered**. But pollution and changes in climate may put them at risk in the future.

**nerve**—a thin strand in the body
   that carries messages
**endangered**—at risk of dying out

# Enemies of Anemones

Tentacles don't protect sea anemones from all **predators**. The animal's sting does not bother butterflyfish or mosshead sculpins. They peck away at an anemone's tentacles. Loggerhead sea turtles devour sea anemones in one gulp. Sea stars, sea slugs, and snails also attack anemones.

**predator**—an animal that hunts another animal for food

# Sea Anemone Life Cycle

Sea anemones release **reproductive cells**. The cells meet in the water. Then they grow into **larvae**. The larvae drift until they attach to a solid object. Then they grow into flowery **polyps**. Slowly the polyps get larger as they become adults.

**Fact!** Sometimes the polyps separate, making two anemones. This is called fission.

larva

reproductive cell—a male or female cell
  needed to make offspring
larva—a stage of development between egg
  and adult
polyp—a small sea animal with a tubular body
  and a round mouth surrounded by tentacles

19

# Amazing But True!

Some sea anemones have a special relationship with clownfish. The anemones' sting does not harm clownfish. A layer of mucus on a clownfish's skin protects it from stings. Predators won't bother the fish when it's hiding in the tentacles. In return, the anemone gets bits of food dropped by the fish.

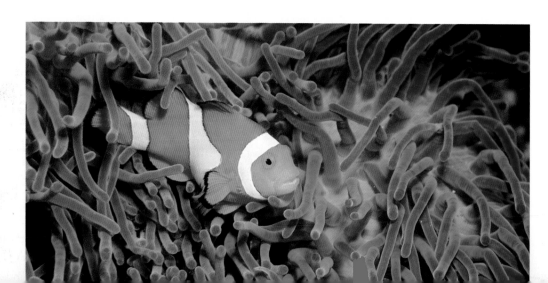

# Sea Anemone Facts

**Where it lives:** oceans worldwide

**Habitat:** found in all ocean habitats, usually among coral reefs

**Size:** 0.5 inch (1.3 cm) to more than 6 feet (1.8 m) wide

**Diet:** plankton, krill, crabs, shrimp, fish, bits of food left by other animals

**Predators:** sea turtles, fish, sea stars, sea slugs, sea snails

**Life span:** 60 to 80 years

**Status:** stable (not at risk of dying out)

tentacle

mouth

column (body)

pedal disc

# Glossary

**algae** (AL-jee)—small plantlike organisms without roots or stems that grow in water or on damp surfaces

**coral reef** (KOR-uhl REEF)—a part of the seafloor made up of the hardened bodies of corals; corals are small, colorful sea creatures

**endangered** (in-DAYN-juhrd)—at risk of dying out

**invertebrate** (in-VUR-tuh-bruht)—an animal without a backbone

**larva** (LAR-vuh)—a stage of life between egg and adult

**nerve** (NURV)—a thin strand in the body that carries messages

**plankton** (PLANGK-tuhn)—tiny organisms that drift in the sea

**polyp** (PAH-lupp)—a small sea animal with a tubular body and a round mouth surrounded by tentacles

**predator** (PRED-uh-tur)—an animal that hunts another animal for food

**prey** (PRAY)—an animal hunted by another animal for food

**reproductive cell** (ree-pruh-DUCK-tiv SELL)—a male or female cell needed to make offspring

**species** (SPEE-sheez)—a group of creatures that are capable of reproducing with one another

**tentacle** (TEN-tuh-kuhl)—a long, armlike body part of some animals

**venom** (VEN-uhm)—a poison an animal makes to kill its prey

# Read More

**Laplante, Walter**. *Sea Anemones*. Things That Sting. Gareth Stevens Publishing, 2015.

**Magby, Meryl**. *Sea Anemones*. Under the Sea. Powerkids Press, 2012.

**Rustad, Martha**. *Clownfish and Sea Anemones Work Together*. Animals Working Together. Capstone Press, 2011.

# Internet Sites

FactHound offers a safe, fun way to find Internet sites related to this book. All of the sites on FactHound have been researched by our staff.

Here's all you do:

Visit *www.facthound.com*

Type in this code: 9781515721390

 Super-cool stuff! Check out projects, games and lots more at **www.capstonekids.com**

# Critical Thinking Using the Common Core

**1.** Name a sea anemone body part and describe how it helps the animal survive. (Key Idea and Details)

**2.** Reread the text on page 6. Then find two photos of sea anemones in this book. Describe how the two anemones are different. Then describe what likenesses they have that make them both sea anemones. (Integration of Knowledge and Ideas)

**3.** Reread the text on page 12. What if the sea anemone did not have a pedal disc? What would be different about its life? (Craft and Structure)

# Index